METAPHORS IN MOTION

Wisdom from the Open Road

TIM AND DEBBIE BISHOP

OPEN ROAD PRESS

Publisher's Note

Certain portions of this text retell stories that originally appeared in *Two Are Better*, which is a memoir also published by Open Road Press and written by the same authors. Whereas *Two Are Better* communicates a life story, *Metaphors in Motion* emphasizes life lessons learned from the Bishops' long-distance bicycle tours. Any duplicate accounts presented in this publication are for the purpose of instruction and personal application.

This publication is designed to teach, enlighten, and inspire.

This print edition, published in 2019 as a service to readers, contains the content that was published in e-book form in 2013. The only changes to that content were made to convert an e-book to a print format. A dedication was added to honor the kindness modeled by the author of this book's foreword, who passed away before the publication of its print edition.

Copyright © 2016 by Timothy G. Bishop and Deborah L. Bishop
All photography herein copyright © Timothy G. Bishop and
Deborah L. Bishop

All rights reserved
No portion of this book may be reproduced, stored in a retrieval system, or transmitted in any form or by any means—electronic, mechanical, photocopy, recording, scanning, or other—except for brief quotations in critical reviews or articles, without the prior written permission of the publisher.

Published in Thompson's Station, Tennessee, USA by Open Road Press.
www.openroadpress.com
First Edition

Scripture taken from the New King James Version®.
Copyright © 1982 by Thomas Nelson, Inc.
Used by permission. All rights reserved.

Library of Congress Control Number: 2019902116
Print edition ISBN: 978-0-9856248-8-0
E-book edition ISBN: 978-0-9856248-5-9

Front cover design by Micah Kandros
Copyediting by Kevin Miller
Proofreading by John David Kudrick

TheHopeLine®, as referred to in this book, is a registered trademark of The Shepherd's Call, Inc.

Tom Nenadal (1952 – 2019)

We dedicate this book to God's servants everywhere who, like Tom Nenadal, come to the aid of travelers in need with no expectations in return. We will always treasure such acts of kindness.

CONTENTS

Foreword vii

Introduction 1

Lesson 1. Over-preparing or Underperforming? 3

Lesson 2. Interstate Adventure 7

Lesson 3. The Road Less Traveled 11

Lesson 4. Choose Faith, Not Fear 15

Lesson 5. Overcoming Inertia 19

Lesson 6. Brand-new Day 23

Lesson 7. Do You Believe in Miracles? 27

Lesson 8. Perseverance Pays Off 31

Topical Index 37

Geographical Index 39

Acknowledgments 41

About the Authors 43

FOREWORD

I can still remember the day Tim and Debbie Bishop walked into my bicycle shop in Marshall, Missouri. It was September 9, 2014, and they were midway across America on their tour in support of TheHopeLine. They had come in for help with a mechanical problem. Just five months earlier, I had taken my bicycling hobby to the next level by opening the shop. Yet as the Bishops walked through my door, I was still wondering if running a bicycle shop was what I was supposed to be doing with my life, or whether there was something more. The timing of their visit fed my soul-searching.

These two travelers weren't the usual type of bicyclists I see coming in and out of my shop every day. They were a bit older than most of my patrons, and they were on a mission. Almost immediately, they began telling me about TheHopeLine and its efforts to help young people in crisis. I could tell they believed deeply in the cause they were promoting and the values underpinning it. They might have suffered from a lack of mechanical know-how, but they had no deficiency in passion and conviction. It seemed their tour was about more than simply checking off another bicycle route from their bucket list.

I helped them with their brakes and then with a navigational problem I knew they would soon be facing. Unbeknownst to them, a bridge on their upcoming route was out. I called a friend who knew exactly how to reroute them. Although I enjoyed lending a hand, I couldn't help but wonder if the reason for our brief encounter was more than merely helping them on their way. Today, as I pen this foreword for two people whom I've come to know well mostly by reading about them, I'm inclined to believe there was more to our meeting than met the eye.

FOREWORD

As you can see, I've stayed in touch with the Bishops. They asked me to read their "life lessons" manuscript before they published it. If you have questions and concerns about your life, your relationships, and God, then reading their material can help you process your options. It may change your outlook, answer some of your questions, and give you hope for a more meaningful life. Just as the Bishops' arrival at my bike shop on that day prompted some deeper thought about a greater purpose in my life, I suspect you'll find that the same will be true for you as you read their stories.

The lessons that follow here in *Metaphors in Motion: Wisdom from the Open Road* will give you a taste of what's in their larger book of life lessons, which they've called *Wheels of Wisdom: Life Lessons for the Restless Spirit*. I, too, have toured long distances by bicycle. It's easy for me to see correlations between cycling across country and some important life issues, including spiritual ones. Both cycling and a faith walk are filled with adventure, excitement, wonder, awe, personal growth, tremendous work, tough decisions—and, sometimes, detours, pain, and disappointment. These experiences help us grow. The Bishops' lessons clearly draw the correlations that will promote your own growth. The questions at the end of each lesson will provoke some important thought that can benefit people of any age.

I invite you to join this journey with the Bishops and grow with each lesson along the way.

Tom Nenadal
Owner, Back from the Past Bicycles
Marshall, Missouri

INTRODUCTION

We're Tim and Debbie Bishop. The book you're about to read is the result of a surprise nugget discovered during the refining process for *Wheels of Wisdom: Life Lessons for the Restless Spirit*, our larger book of life lessons from the open road. While we labored to turn *Wheels* into a polished piece that could shine in the literary marketplace, our reviewers and editors were saying the same thing: "It's too big. You need to pare out some lessons." However, few of those people were ready to nominate which of the sixty lessons we should presumably discard. "They're all good!" was the common response of our editors.

Soon, it became apparent that we shouldn't discard any of them, but rather we should share eight lessons in this book while leaving fifty-two others, conveniently coinciding with the number of weeks in a year, in *Wheels of Wisdom*. The ultimate criteria for removing lessons from *Wheels of Wisdom* were not premised on identifying weak lessons. That would have been very subjective, because the collective feedback from our reviewers suggested no clear losers. Reviewers seemed to have their own unique favorites. Instead, we looked for lessons that conveyed similar principles, told a similar story, or were cast in similar settings. Rest assured, you're not about to read "the rejects."

Some background is in order before you embark with us on this virtual journey. First, we were lifelong singles until marrying at age fifty-two. Since both of us had been entrenched in long-term careers before marrying, a bicycling adventure seemed like the perfect way to begin our new life together. To our surprise, our bicycle trip from Oregon to Maine in the summer of 2010, coupled with our major midlife changes, brought new insights to the forefront. We toured twice more in the years leading up to this book, and we found that each adventure brought a new perspective and fresh insights to life. We learned some of these life principles anew, while we encountered others for the first time. Regardless, we thought these lessons compelling enough to offer them to others.

The stories in *Metaphors in Motion* come from two of our long-distance tours: our "honeymoon on wheels" and TheHopeLine Tour. We share more about our 2010 honeymoon tour in our inaugural book, *Two Are Better: Midlife Newlyweds Bicycle Coast to Coast*. In 2014, we cycled across America yet again and dedicated that tour to raising awareness and funds for TheHopeLine, a cause that is dear to our hearts as volunteer Hope Coaches. To date, we've toured over ten thousand miles. In addition to what you'll see in this book, we have many more photos and some videos at www.openroadpress.com.

Each lesson that follows comes with some personal reflection questions to help you apply the principles to your own life. You may want to keep a pencil and some paper handy as you consider what each lesson could mean to you personally.

Thank you for joining us. While we hope you find the stories engaging, we also hope you discover some important takeaways. Enjoy the ride!

LESSON 1

Over-preparing or Underperforming?

Over-preparing can be a sure sign faith is losing the battle with fear.

By Tim

Every now and then when you are touring by bicycle, it can be helpful to check into a bike shop. It's even better when you have some minor issue with your bicycle as you approach one, because it may be a sign you need to stop. On TheHopeLine Tour, we'd cycled many miles with no bicycle shops around for days, so when my left brake handle started acting up after ninety days on the road, it seemed prudent to have the bicycles checked out.

The mechanic at the bike shop in downtown Delaware, Ohio, troubleshot my brake problem quickly. As good mechanics do, he also found other issues neither Debbie nor I would have found, and fixed them before they caused trouble miles away from services.

While he worked on our bikes, he asked about our tour. It wasn't long before we admitted to our deficiency with mechanical matters, which prompted him to say, "Anyone who goes on a tour of this magnitude should be able to completely tear down and rebuild his own bike."

His comment was probably spoken from his strength as a mechanic, but it struck a sour chord within this non-mechanic. I didn't challenge his assertion, but I knew it wasn't true. We'd already been on two long tours before TheHopeLine Tour and made it home to tell about them. We'd not had a roadside crisis requiring intensive mechanical expertise, but if we had, I don't think we'd have been stranded in the middle of nowhere without somebody coming to our assistance.

I reflected on his comment throughout that day. I still think it illustrates why many people do not pursue their goals and dreams. Sometimes, over-preparing is just an excuse for underperforming.

The prior day, we had met a pleasant couple on a bike path in London, Ohio. They were in their early seventies and still riding long distances on their recumbent bicycles. The man didn't have many regrets about his life, but he did regret not bicycling across America. He said he was too much of a chicken. I didn't let on to him that I was a chicken too. Touring with Debbie made all the difference for me. Regardless, this spry couple had decided not to let age and long distances away from doctors get in their way.

You can't have everything lined up in perfect order before going on a bicycle trip—or pursuing any other worthwhile dream. We all have different strengths and weaknesses as well as an inability to control what goes on around us. Imperfection comes with being human.

Rather than focusing on our limitations and allowing them to hold us back, Debbie and I allowed our passion to fuel our touring pursuits and then acquired the missing expertise along the way. We exercised reasonable precautions, like buying reliable equipment and stopping at a bike shop periodically for preventative maintenance. In the end, however, we needed to trust God for those things we couldn't anticipate or control. Otherwise, we would never have aspired to or been willing to pursue any adventure. This approach applies to anyone's journey, regardless of the dream or the calling.

It takes humility to ask for help, and you'll usually find help right around the next corner simply waiting for the request. Just-in-time guidance is part of God's provision as you walk in obedience with the passions He's given you. No one can achieve their dreams without help from other people. When you involve others, you honor them.

Therefore, in spite of our expert mechanic's advice, we wouldn't be learning how to tear down and rebuild our bicycles anytime soon. Although it might have been interesting and helpful, we were too busy trying to pedal them—and trying to raise awareness and funds for TheHopeLine. That's what we'd been called to do.

What about you? What are you called to do? Are you over-preparing *and* underperforming? It may be time for some frank self-talk before your dreams pass you by.

You'll never be 100 percent prepared for what you might encounter in pursuit of your goals. Spending time anticipating every problem that may arise is time better spent on discovering the problems firsthand and then putting your problem-solving skills to good use. If you've already done the bulk of your planning, chances are you're about to become stuck or you already are. It's time to quit stalling and begin the adventure!

And the Lord said to Moses, "Why do you cry to Me? Tell the children of Israel to go forward."

Exodus 14:15

Personal Reflection:
1. What have you been planning to do for so long that you're wondering if it will ever happen?
2. Think of a recent endeavor that you needed to prepare for. At what point did your preparations translate into stalling?
3. How might you design your next plan to allow for changes to the plan after implementing it?

METAPHORS IN MOTION

Chasing dreams north of Columbus, Ohio

LESSON 2

Interstate Adventure

At times, we meet resistance because we don't recognize or heed wise advice. Nevertheless, mercy and grace abound.

By Tim

Perhaps you're familiar with the proverbial horse that is led to water but refuses to drink. Well, shame on me for asking for advice outside of Bozeman, Montana, on TheHopeLine Tour and then deciding not to follow it. We'd been on the road twenty-five days and had decided to leave the TransAmerica Trail in favor of what we thought would be a better route for us. That meant we'd need some help improvising our routing until we met up with Adventure Cycling Association's Lewis & Clark Trail.

The following morning started innocently enough. We rode the I-90 frontage road from Belgrade to Bozeman following the directions I'd received the prior evening from a tech-savvy motel receptionist. Once in Bozeman, however, I began to doubt the route ahead. The interstate seemed to offer a more direct path to our intended destination, and the climb through Bozeman Pass would be much more gradual than on secondary roads. We also wanted to avoid what we suspected would be a cumbersome ride on a gravel road.

After discussing the matter, we decided to go to the local AAA office and inquire about road conditions and routes. By then, we were more or less convinced we'd use the highway, despite one person's attempt to talk us out of it. We also wanted a tour book for upcoming routing and accommodation questions.

Eventually, we made it to the AAA office, where we had warm and engaging conversations with the local staff. We shared about TheHopeLine and our story before running another errand and then riding through downtown to see the sights. We anticipated Bozeman to be the largest city we would encounter for miles to come.

Finally, we hopped on the interstate and embarked on our trip out of town. It wasn't long before I began questioning my recommendation to deviate from the bicycle route map the motel receptionist had so kindly provided. Traffic was more robust than on our last venture onto I-90 a few days earlier, and the shoulder became narrower and narrower the longer we rode. A gravel road would have been better.

Once on the highway, we couldn't very well reverse our direction or our decision. As the shoulder shrank and the rumble strips disappeared, we were wedged around a couple of bends for our final ascent up Bozeman Pass, with tractor-trailers whizzing by at eighty miles per hour. Eventually, the shoulder returned to an acceptable width, but not before much anxiety and trepidation.

I-90 east of Bozeman, Montana

The interstate adventure had its redeeming qualities, among them beautiful views and a gradual climb. However, if I had known about the traffic and road conditions, we would never have gone there. The advantages didn't outweigh the stress of tolerating the adverse conditions or the risk to our well-being.

In any choice in life, if we only knew what an option would be like, it would make our decision of whether or not to try it so much easier. We can gather information from others with more experience or research options ourselves, but there will still be factors unknown to us until we actually see them for ourselves. That's where faith comes in. We do our best and leave the rest up to God.

God has given us free will to choose the path we travel. In His grace, He often provides us guidance to make our travels safer and more pleasurable. In hindsight, I think God had already provided His divine guidance the previous night at the motel, if only I had recognized it. Nevertheless, we get to choose. And even though we may not choose the best path God has intended for us, He can bless our journey anyway. That's just the way He is.

The Lord is merciful and gracious, slow to anger, and abounding in mercy.

Psalm 103:8

Personal Reflection:
1. Recall a time when you didn't heed good advice and paid a price for it. Why did you go against the advice you were given?
2. Do you have trouble trusting your decisions—or even making them—when you face the unknown?
3. Think of three possible sources of wisdom for the next time you face a difficult decision. For example, whom might you consult, what might you read, and what other investigation can you perform?

METAPHORS IN MOTION

Destination unknown outside Culdesac, Idaho

LESSON 3

The Road Less Traveled

Despite the best of planning, you will experience a learning curve on your life pursuits. The advice of others will help, but you'll want a Guide who goes before you and can see through dark places that you cannot.

By Debbie

One of the best things about bicycle touring is the amount of food we can enjoy without worrying about caloric intake. On day nine of our honeymoon tour, I had a huge steak cooked to perfection at Donald's Café in Lapwai, Idaho. It was delicious! I enjoyed every bite while Tim and I listened to local wisdom about which road we should take after dinner. Another benefit of touring is the openness of the locals to give us advice on roads they know so well. They have roadworthy knowledge we can't glean even from studying our trusty maps.

"You should stay off the main road," one man said. "Some bicyclists have died on that stretch of road."

No one needed to say more. Taking the road less traveled would be safer, though considerably steeper and longer, than the more traveled route. Slow and safe sounded better than fast and dangerous. At least a campground in Winchester provided us with a destination.

Sunlight burns into late evening during summer in the Pacific Northwest. By the time we had set out from our delightful dinner at Donald's, however, we had only a few hours before darkness would descend and force us to stop for the evening.

As we ascended Old Winchester Grade Road, the sun slipped down toward the distant western horizon. We witnessed such beauty as we glanced behind us. I will never forget that sight. The afterglow seemed to last much longer than usual. We were higher up and could see colorful effects over the many rolling hills as the orange deepened into darkness. Had we been able to reach out and touch those hills, surely they would have been as soft as velvet.

Sunset on Old Winchester Grade Road in Idaho

Later, on TheHopeLine Tour in Montana, someone warned us to be cautious of road names that included the word *grade*. In Idaho on that first tour, Old Winchester Grade Road proved to be winding and steep. As darkness overcame us, we couldn't see just how steep it was, but we could sure feel it. At least the darkness masked the perilous drop-off on the edge of the road. No guardrails were there to stop us should we wander too close to the edge. Yet we were going so slowly that we wouldn't fall overboard even if a passing car pushed us toward the brink.

Into the night we pedaled, slowly and cautiously. Soon, we strapped on our headlamps and continued uphill. We had no idea how far away our campground was, nor could we foresee the condition of the road ahead. We were truly riding by blind faith despite the narrow rays of light from our headlamps. I was exhausted and terrified, but I did not want Tim to know how I felt. Our first major marital conflict a few days earlier was still fresh in my mind.

As we continued ever so slowly uphill, I asked God repeatedly to make Tim stop somewhere along the road so we could quit for the night. There were few homes and, thankfully, no cars as we ascended, only the two of us shrouded in darkness. I thought we could knock on someone's door, if we found a home with lights on. However, none appeared. I kept praying.

Finally, after what seemed like an hour's worth of riding in the dark, Tim scouted out a parcel of land on which to rest our tired bodies. It was ten thirty. I didn't have to yell, scream, or threaten. He stopped, and we set up camp in the starlight.

We'll remember that night all the days of our lives. Not only did we have the most memorable sunset as we ascended Old Winchester Grade Road, we also had fresh air, clear sky, and myriad shining stars showering us with gratitude. Perseverance always pays off. Although we did not make it to our destination, we had given it our best shot. We stopped at the perfect place, on a priceless section of land. As inexperienced and exhausted campers, we did not consider any of the risks we later thought of in hindsight. Bears, coyotes, wolves, and mountain lions most likely frequented that area. Thankfully, we were naïve enough to neglect such hazards, and the creatures of the night gave us a free pass. We slept more peacefully than many of the nights we rested in motels.

All of us are on a journey in life, and road conditions vary. Sometimes, the road is straight, flat, smooth, and free from potholes. Other times, it is rough and dangerous, curvy and uphill. Regardless, we only make progress when we keep traveling forward, even if we lack confidence or fear a wreck. Joy in the journey is always possible no matter how difficult the terrain, because God can go before us and guide us. Even if we find ourselves on the road less traveled, He makes all things possible. His light shines in the darkness as we choose to trust Him.

If I say, "Surely the darkness shall fall on me," even the night shall be light about me; indeed, the darkness shall not hide from You, but the night shines as the day; the darkness and the light are both alike to You.

Psalm 139:11-12

Personal Reflection:
1. When you face a task that instills fear, how do you address your fear?
2. Do you think God can allay your fears? If so, how?
3. If you were to ask God for help when you become anxious or fearful while pursuing a worthy goal, what would you ask Him to do?

LESSON 4

Choose Faith, Not Fear

Faith is the opposite of fear and an antidote for it. Recalling past successes will bolster faith whenever fear rears its ugly head.

By Tim

TheHopeLine Tour was intense but rewarding. We covered a lot of ground and had to get creative upon occasion with the route. By the seventy-sixth day, we had made our way into the southeastern quadrant of Missouri on Adventure Cycling Association's Great Rivers South route.

Typical lettered road in Missouri

Two days earlier, we couldn't wait to get away from that route. It was sending us farther into Ozark country, which was beautiful but also had narrow roads, steep hills, and few services. We'd had enough of that. We managed to escape the narrow roads and the hills, but how would we find our way back to the prescribed safe route? How would we get to Cape Girardeau and back onto the ACA maps to find our way farther east?

We began our quest meandering on lettered roads under overcast skies. In Missouri, if a route is denoted with one letter (e.g., A) or a double letter (e.g., AA), it is a paved road with no shoulder and, often, light traffic. They call them "highways" (e.g., AA Highway), and you can count on plenty of rolling hills and some curves thrown in for good measure. Such was the case again as we attempted our return to the designated route.

After sixty-odd miles, we arrived in Jackson, a sizeable suburb of Cape Girardeau, as evening rush hour dawned. We needed to get off the shoulder-less lettered highways, because traffic had become more congested. I asked a lady outside a local store for advice.

"How many miles have you guys gone?" she asked.

"Three thousand! We started in Oregon," I replied.

"Why would anyone do such a thing? I'm active, and I like exercise, but I'll do it at the gym. Aren't you concerned about people texting while they drive?" She proceeded to inform us that her husband, who spent eight years in the legislature, was unable to get a bill passed to regulate cell phone use by Missouri drivers.

"Does this road have any shoulders on it? Is it okay to bicycle on?" I asked while pointing to the adjacent, four-lane Kings Highway, which had begun filling up with cars transporting tired and hungry workers to their evening escape.

Her eyes widened. "You're going to bicycle on *that* road?"

Eventually, we determined Kings Highway would be our safest route into Cape Girardeau. We did so without explaining to the lady that we had bicycled through a detour on an interstate in Montana on the left-hand, three-foot shoulder into oncoming traffic. Although we were concerned about the traffic and the narrow shoulder on Kings Highway, we'd seen far worse. When confronting risk on the road, Debbie and I would assess the situation, collaboratively make our best judgment, exercise caution, and then leave the rest up to God. This woman's tolerance for this type of risk and her choice to avoid it clearly differed from ours.

Debbie and I hope to use the same decision-making model with any issues we face in life. If we avoid all risk, where is the adventure—or the faith? Recognizing that many things are beyond our control and placing our trust in the One who loves us and has a plan for our lives seems like the best approach. If we let our fears rule us, we'll never reach our full potential.

How do you decide about "traveling on crowded highways" in your own life? Do you rely on experiences that have already prepared you to cope with challenging situations, or do you avoid the difficult roads altogether? If you dwell on only the hazards and allow them to decide for you, you'll shortchange your adventure. With God's help, you're already equipped to accomplish more than you thought possible. So choose faith, not fear.

Now faith is the substance of things hoped for, the evidence of things not seen.

Hebrews 11:1

Personal Reflection:
1. Do you agree with the statement, "Faith is the opposite of fear"? Why or why not?
2. Why do some people fear things that others don't?
3. What is the biggest fear in your life? How can you develop a different approach to that fear to find confidence and comfort?

METAPHORS IN MOTION

Alive!

LESSON 5

Overcoming Inertia

No matter where you are in life, there's always a better future. But first, you must overcome inertia.

By Tim

When you travel by bicycle, you see a world brimming with a variety of lifestyles, living conditions, and opportunities for personal growth. Rich, poor, and in-between, we saw it all on our ride through Cleveland on our first tour. Our journey east of the city was particularly striking. Just a few revolutions of our wheels brought us from the posh to the paupers, separated merely by a steel gate and a fence.

When we headed toward downtown in the morning, we cycled from upper-middle-class to lower-middle-class dwellings. Then, we hit the urban dwellings, high-rise apartment buildings surrounded by concrete and commotion. After we exited stage right—east, that is—we were awestruck by the contrast of residential neighborhoods.

We cycled from an industrial park into a wealthy borough of Cleveland. Heavy tree cover shielded us from the sunlight or any big, billowy clouds that may have arisen from the waters of Lake Erie. Ornate fences, lavish landscaping, and elaborate security systems concealed the lucrative homes within. With a lockdown like that, the residents had become inmates in a prison of their own making, or so it seemed to this passerby.

Soon, we left extravagance behind and entered another unfamiliar and uncomfortable world. Narrow lots with rundown houses and an intermittent liquor store surrounded a broad, beaten-up boulevard. Vehicles that could have passed as junkyard reclamations lined the street. Raggedly clad individuals milled about with evidently too much time on their hands, their faces drawn with misery. Instantly, the dial had changed from *Lifestyles of the Rich and Famous* to another sad episode of *Cops*. We simply wanted to avoid being a part of the cast. Instinct substantiated the advice we'd received already, suggesting plenty of "bad boys" frequented that neighborhood.

Were those who lived on that set destined to endure an entire lifetime behind those bars? I wondered if they felt trapped due to their poverty. Or were they unable to see a way out to something better and to pursue it wholeheartedly until they escaped? Clearly, inner joy can reside no matter the surroundings. Yet in my own twisted perception of reality, I couldn't envision living in that setting—or in the one we'd just left.

The diversity of living conditions we'd seen on that day made an impression on me. Along with those conditions came the circumstances that either established them or perpetuated them. The surroundings made me wonder: *How did both of these neighborhoods come about? And what will their future bring?*

Another thought occurred to me: *What does MY world look like?*

Are we all prisoners in our own settings, entrenched in what no longer holds promise for us? Do we know what awaits us "on the other side"? Do we even know there is another side? If we're honest with ourselves, we'll see the potential, if not the need, to break free in some facet of our lives.

I was beginning to appreciate that each of us lives in a world that is relatively small. Some are bigger than others, but all have limited scope. It's hard to comprehend what might become available to us if we are open to expanding our spheres and changing.

Change can be difficult. We all long for security, a basic human need. If our present circumstances are tolerable, it's natural to protect the status quo rather than delve into the unknown. Choosing not to change, however, prevents us from expanding our world. Are we reluctant to try a new hobby at the expense of sacrificing something else we enjoy? Do we accept mediocrity in our work lives rather than striving for something better because we don't want to lose what we already have? Are we willing to move to another location so God can unveil new opportunities to use us and grow us there?

Our bicycle touring has opened my eyes. So many places offer new experiences and new opportunities for those willing to venture forth. Recognizing opportunities may be hard when you view them from your own limited perspective. However, a Higher Power oversees it all. And with an intimate connection to Him, you can trust He will lead you toward a deeper walk with Him and toward a brighter future, no matter the setting. Inevitably, moving forward will require change. You won't progress if you're in neutral. And because the unknown accompanies change, faith is a requirement.

In what avenue of your life have you stopped pedaling, unwilling to reengage and struggling with inertia? Are you wondering why you lack zeal, what went wrong, and whether things will ever change? What if random travelers could look into your life? Would they wonder the same things? If they glanced at your face, would they see someone who looks joyful or miserable? Does it concern you that more years will pass by you and your dreams?

If you could travel forward in time and catch a glimpse of your life five, ten, twenty years down the road, would you want it to look like it does today? Don't allow yourself to get caught in the inertia trap. Walk in faith toward a more fulfilling life. Be intentional about the people with whom you spend your time, what you do in your spare time, what you do for work, and where you live.

Take heart. God's best is waiting for you on the other side of the barbed wire. It's time to plan your escape.

Enlarge the place of your tent, and let them stretch out the curtains of your dwellings; do not spare; lengthen your cords, and strengthen your stakes.

Isaiah 54:2

Personal Reflection:
1. In what area of your life has inertia set in?
2. Brainstorm ways to advance in that area. Consider talking about it with a trusted confidant, taking a trip to the library, doing a Google search to research options, or traveling to a new place to open your eyes to new possibilities.
3. Think of a goal that will help eliminate inertia in this area of your life. Write it down with a target date and then begin pursuing it.

LESSON 6

Brand-new Day

Some days are better than others. When you encounter a difficult day, know that the sun will come up the next day. A new day after some sleep will breathe new life into your journey.

By Debbie

Winston Churchill said it best, "Never, ever, ever give up."

Never give up is the essence of bicycle touring and marriage. I had discovered that firsthand after marrying Tim and cycling over some steep inclines and through some hot weather in the Pacific Northwest on our honeymoon tour.

Churchill also said, "Never give up on something that you can't go a day without thinking about." Well, not a day had gone by without thinking of Tim or our bicycle adventure. Each day, even on the hard ones, loving thoughts about my husband and a memory or scene from our bicycle tour kept popping into my mind. One particular day was etched in my memory for several reasons.

The previous days had been fraught with strife between Tim and me. Tension had been high. So were my expectations of what our trip would be like—maybe a bit too high. Slowly, I was catching on to the hard work and perseverance needed to make it across the country. We had fought in Umatilla, Oregon, two days earlier, and I had said some unkind words. Thankfully, we prayed together before we went to bed that night. We also got some much-needed sleep.

Waking up to a new day was a blessing. If we had given up in Umatilla, we would have headed home with our tails between our legs. I'm grateful neither of us gives up easily. Sometimes, I think when we get so discouraged we don't think we can go on, God gives us a double portion of joy, delight, peace, or whatever we need for the moment. Our part is to stay committed for the long haul.

That day's ride doubled our delight. Its events reminded me yet again *not to quit before the miracle happens.* The fresh, cooler air behind our backs, the billowing wheat fields, the gradual downhill rides, the vast views, and sharing everything together made the past few days of tension evaporate as quickly as the water from my bandanna. We cycled over ninety miles from Walla Walla to Clarkston, Washington. I loved that day. I forgot all about the secret desire I'd been harboring to fly home when we arrived in the next town with an airport.

Growing

God was teaching me some lessons on that trip, none of which I'd have learned had I quit at the first, second, or third difficulty. C. S. Lewis said, "God whispers to us in pleasure and shouts to us in pain." I want to hear from Him at every decibel, and I certainly will if I stay on the course He has set before me.

Tim and I not only read the Bible together, we also read it individually. When I seek the Lord for wisdom in being the woman—and now the wife—He calls me to be, I'm reminded of Proverbs 31: 11-12, which says, "The heart of her husband safely trusts her; so he will have no lack of gain. She does him good and not evil all the days of her life." Now *that* is something to strive for each day, whether traveling on a bicycle trip or through daily life.

> *Through the Lord's mercies we are not consumed, because His compassions fail not. They are new every morning; great is Your faithfulness.*
>
> Lamentations 3:22-23

Personal Reflection:

1. If you're in need of some refreshment today, how can you alter your routine to shake things up? For example, is it time to take a different route home, go to a new place for lunch, or call someone you haven't talked to for months?
2. The next time you are discouraged and tempted to give up, what can you anticipate that will help you persevere?
3. What acquaintance of yours could use a fresh perspective? Consider how you might tactfully encourage him or her to change things up.

METAPHORS IN MOTION

In southeast Missouri, two weeks after Sioux City, Iowa

LESSON 7

Do You Believe in Miracles?

When you pray for the miraculous, do you believe God can make it happen? And will you be bold enough to allow Him to answer your prayers by venturing forth? Before God will help us "walk on water," He usually waits for us to "step out of the boat."

By Tim

Sioux City, Iowa, had been exerting a strong hold on us after 2,300 miles on TheHopeLine Tour, but we finally broke free following our fifteen-day stay to rest Debbie's lower right leg. The doctor had diagnosed her with chronic compartment syndrome with a projected recovery time of one to three months with plenty of rest. As an alternative to packing up and flying home for the long recuperation period and the winter to follow, he said we could rest it and then test it with limited mileage. We opted for some even speedier treatment, combining rest with requests for prayer from a multitude of committed prayer warriors.

Perhaps symbolic of our departure from Sioux City was one of the weirdest sights I have ever seen. It occurred outside the hotel while we prepared our bicycles for a return to the road. Debbie's right foot was visited by an unexpected intruder: a bat! That's right, one of those eerie, web-winged creatures featured in horror movies.

Was this clingy creature an evil icon depicting its last claim to Debbie's injured leg? Or was it symbolic of Sioux City's firm grasp and its reluctance to let us out of its clutches? Regardless, kicking the creepy bat away and leaving it behind mirrored the feeling that came with finally venturing out on the road and leaving Sioux City behind. We felt liberated.

When we departed, however, we still had questions and concerns about Debbie's leg. It had improved somewhat during our rest period, but she hadn't been consistently pain free. Even on the night before we left, I was applying thumb pressure on her lower leg, at her direction, because I had no idea how deep-tissue massage works or if it would even work at all for an injury like hers. When we went to bed, Debbie said, "My leg still isn't right."

At our stop in Whiting—after a tailwind had pushed us thirty miles down a pancake-flat road—she said she couldn't believe it. Her leg didn't hurt! When I heard the same report at day's end, it seemed a miracle had happened. Six more weeks of pain-free cycling proved it!

The timing of our miracle came with an added bonus—I suppose to enhance the outpouring of blessings all the more. On the day before we left, we avoided a wild storm with eighty-mile-per-hour winds merely ten miles to the southeast. When we rode through that area, people were busy cleaning up debris. The storm had uprooted trees, strewn large branches everywhere, and damaged several roofs. Good Samaritans were out in full force, as scattered about as the fallen branches, extending kindness in the cleanup effort to strangers who had suffered damage to their property. The goodwill warmed our hearts.

Sometimes, I wonder why we pray, and ask others to pray, if we don't trust that God can heal us. When the answer to those prayers comes as asked, why are we so surprised? Is it a measure of our underestimating faith, or are we so scientifically wired that we no longer believe in miracles? And why do we try to explain away what has happened in ways that we can understand and accept?

In our case, we could say that the doctor misdiagnosed chronic compartment syndrome or its recovery timetable. On the other hand, we could admit that the details prompting his

DO YOU BELIEVE IN MIRACLES?

advice were irrelevant. Debbie's condition and his treatment plan slowed us down from an unsustainable pace. We gained much-needed rest and made many connections with people on the fundraising aspects of our tour. Debbie even had time to engineer some great-looking signs for our bicycles!

Ultimately, we cycled 4,300 miles and raised over $32,000 on TheHopeLine Tour. I'd say the doctor's diagnosis and the treatment plan were right on the money, exactly in keeping with God's will. It was a miracle! And, as comical as it seemed at the time, the bat sighting further validated the supernatural nature of our Sioux City interlude.

Have you been praying for your own miracle but have yet to see it happen? At some point, you need to stop praying—and waiting—and simply step out in faith. Otherwise, you could be stuck indefinitely, mired under the faulty impression that God hasn't heard your prayers. He has heard them. He may simply be waiting for you to take some action so He can show you.

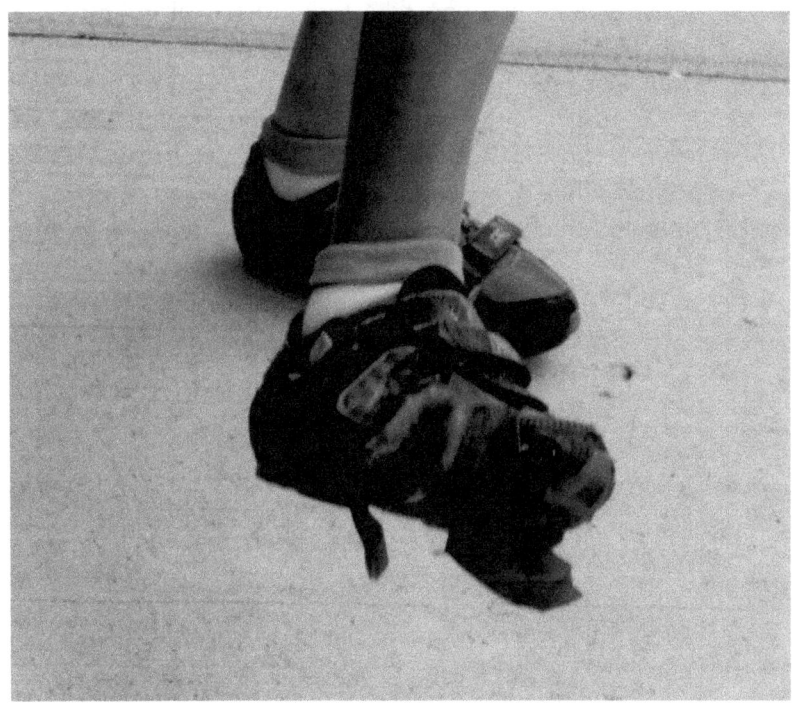

Explain this!

Often, God allows us the blessing of participating in our own miracles, if not helping to make them happen. The story He wants to give you will be compelling for the people you tell. By exercising some faith and taking action, you're demonstrating a relationship with God that others need to see. It's an integral part of the miracle. God may still choose to perform the miraculous without your help, but He wants you to show just how much you believe.

> *Jesus said to him, "If you can believe, all things are possible to him who believes." Immediately the father of the child cried out and said with tears, "Lord, I believe; help my unbelief!"*
>
> Mark 9:23-24

Personal Reflection:
1. Do you want proof of miracles, or can you accept them at face value?
2. What actions can you take today that will indicate you believe God can perform the miracle you've been seeking?
3. If you can't come up with any actions, brainstorm with a trusted confidant. Your miracle may be around the next corner, and you want to be prepared to claim it.

LESSON 8

Perseverance Pays Off

The reward of an endeavor often parallels the amount of sweat required to attain it. Give your pursuits all the effort, enthusiasm, and energy you can muster. You won't be disappointed.

By Tim

After surpassing the one-thousand-mile barrier on TheHopeLine Tour, Debbie and I felt good about things. However, not every day goes as planned or is as easy as you hope. You shouldn't take life's blessings for granted.

On day twenty-three of our tour, we had two choices: ride frontage roads and the interstate, or travel Montana Route 1. Each path led to the same destination but arrived there from opposite directions, circumventing the mountain range in between. Neither of us wanted to ride the interstate again, as we had the day before, so we opted for Route 1 through Flint Creek Pass.

Soon, substandard road conditions, a stiff headwind, and gravity threatened to sour our experience. Travel was slow and discouraging. Sights of snow on distant mountains, denoting the Continental Divide, kept our flagging energy flickering. Those hills would grow larger and closer as the day wore on. First, though, after twenty-eight miles, we landed in the town of Philipsburg, which diverted our attention from the adverse travel conditions.

Philipsburg is a small town with some western culture and style. People were gathering for a weekend celebration. After lunch at a barbecue joint, we visited a candy store—but not just any candy store. This candy store had some scale to it, coated with a healthy layer of nostalgia, given the décor and selections.

In the center of the store, glassed-in cases filled with multicolored candies of the day and the sweetest treats from yesteryear drew a throng of sweet-toothed patrons—including us—into the shop. Lining the walls were countless bins brimming with treats. Above them were shelves loaded with glass jars, each with their own unique contents. Excited children shot to and fro as if injected with a large dose of the goods within. Debbie joined in the revelry while I took pictures of it.

This confectionery unapologetically spared no sugar. Supersized mounds of chocolate would surely tantalize recovering chocoholics while heightening and prolonging their euphoria. The multitude of sweet sights provided a worthy and delectable intermission to the day's adventure. We felt like we'd returned to childhood. Neither of us was in a hurry to leave, especially given the drain in energy that had brought us there. The setting revived us.

With many miles beckoning and a mountain to climb before we would reach our destination, we pulled ourselves away from the glee and returned to the road. Several miles later, we turned east and escaped the headwind. Cycling without wind resistance was a welcome relief, but the pace of travel picked up for only a few miles, because a sharper climb awaited us.

Soon, we were crawling up a steep incline replete with switchbacks. Flint Creek Pass is a tight mountain pass with limited shoulders. Concrete barriers separated us from a plunging gorge merely a few feet to our right. The views at higher altitude began to convert our discouragement to awe and wonder. The adjacent cliffs and gorge were spellbinding. We gazed over miles of forest and the winding road we had just navigated. Even what we supposed to be a fledgling, clandestine artist had adopted this pass. He or she had carved a large heart out of the trees on a facing hill, reminding us, of course, of one another. The reasons why we like to tour by bicycle were popping up all around us. Our perseverance was paying off.

Once atop Flint Creek Pass, we enjoyed captivating views of the hills surrounding Georgetown Lake, a man-made reservoir designed to exploit the latent power of snowmelt at altitude. Magnificent scenery filled the remainder of our ride. Better yet, we discovered easy downhill cycling with what had become a tailwind. We cycled effortlessly for miles until we arrived in Anaconda. It's amazing how quickly your fortunes can change when you stick to your mission and don't give up.

Rolling into a fully booked town meant camping in the city park. However, after a beautiful day like that one, camping didn't sound so bad.

The spoils

We're quite certain that the views—and even the candy—on that day looked more appealing because of the effort required to discover them. When you embrace a challenging endeavor wholeheartedly and then near the finish line, chances are the bounty will appear as grand as the mountains we saw that day and will exhilarate you. Easy pickings, on the other hand, bring little reward. They will look uninviting and taste bland. Yet when you reach far and give your pursuit all you have, the prize will rival the size of Montana's big sky. The most significant benefit, of course, will be the satisfaction you feel. The longer and more difficult the struggle, the greater the fulfillment.

A desire accomplished is sweet to the soul.

Proverbs 13:19a

Personal Reflection:
1. What are some specific reasons why you limit your efforts on certain endeavors?
2. Do you lack satisfaction in your life? If so, what changes are you willing to make to obtain greater fulfillment?
3. Are you on an adventure right now, but you're not giving it your all? What can you do to make it a grand adventure?

AN INVITATION

Please help other readers discover this book by leaving a review on your favorite bookseller's website or on Goodreads.com. For more life lessons from the Bishops, check out their award-winning book, *Wheels of Wisdom: Life Lessons for the Restless Spirit*, online or at a bookseller near you. Here's what others are saying about *Wheels of Wisdom*:

"A road map for life."
—*Publishers Weekly*

"Extremely readable and thought-provoking."
—Dr. John Giannini, former head men's basketball coach, La Salle University

"Sage advice for people at all stages of life."
—Jim Sayer, Executive Director, Adventure Cycling

"Practical ... great design ... excellent!"
—Constance Rhodes, CEO, FINDING*balance*

"A reminder that we are all privileged travelers in this world of wonder."
—Dan Miller, *New York Times* bestselling author

TOPICAL INDEX

A
Action: Lessons 1, 2, 7
Adventure: Lesson 3
Anxiety: Lesson 2

B
Blessings: Lessons 3, 6, 7, 8

C
Challenges: Lesson 8
Change: Lessons 5, 8
Choices: Lesson 2
Counsel: Lessons 2, 3

D
Deciding: Lessons 2, 4
Difficult circumstances: Lessons 5, 6, 8
Discernment: Lesson 3
Discouragement: Lesson 8
Doubt: Lesson 2

E
Encouragement: Lesson 6
Expectations: Lesson 6

F
Faith: Lessons 1, 2, 4, 5, 7
Fear: Lessons 1, 3, 4

G
Good Samaritans: Lesson 7
Grace: Lessons 2, 3
Gratitude: Lesson 3
Guidance: Lessons 2, 3

H
Humility: Lesson 1

L
Letting go: Lesson 4

M
Marriage: Lesson 6
Mercy: Lesson 2
Miracles: Lesson 7

O
Opportunity: Lesson 5

P
Perseverance: Lessons 3, 6, 8
Prayer: Lessons 3, 7
Protection: Lesson 4
Providence: Lesson 7

R
Renewal: Lessons 6, 7
Rest: Lessons 6, 7

TOPICAL INDEX

S

Satisfaction: Lesson 8
Spiritual darkness: Lesson 7
Stuck: Lessons 1, 5, 7

T

Testing: Lesson 7
TheHopeLine: Introduction
Timing: Lesson 7

U

Underperforming: Lesson 1

W

Worrying: Lesson 1

GEOGRAPHICAL INDEX

Legend:
 HW = 2010 Honeymoon on Wheels
 HLT = TheHopeLine Tour of 2014

Idaho
Culdesac, The Road Less Traveled (HW, Lesson 3)

Iowa
Sioux City, Do You Believe in Miracles? (HLT, Lesson 7)

Missouri
Jackson, Choose Faith, Not Fear (HLT, Lesson 4)

Montana
Bozeman Pass, Interstate Adventure (HLT, Lesson 2)
Flint Creek Pass, Perseverance Pays Off (HLT, Lesson 8)

Ohio
Delaware, Over-preparing or Underperforming? (HLT, Lesson 1)
Cleveland, Overcoming Inertia (HW, Lesson 5)

Washington
Clarkston, Brand-new Day (HW, Lesson 6)

ACKNOWLEDGMENTS

In addition to the contributors who read early versions of the *Wheels of Wisdom* manuscript and are listed in the acknowledgments for that book, the following individuals were particularly helpful to the *Metaphors in Motion* project: Jessica Bishop, Christie Hagerman, David Harbison, Kaylea Harbison, Mary Harbison, Fred Ludwig, Kathy McHenry, Heather Randall, and Sarah Williams. Thank you for helping us decipher which lessons had a similar feel.

Thanks as well to the following content, design, and editorial contributors: Micah Kandros, John David Kudrick, Kevin Miller, and Tom Nenadal.

Life Got You Down?
Need Help?

If you're 13-29 years old, reach out now at www.thehopeline.com/gethelp/.

IT MAY JUST SAVE YOUR LIFE.

ABOUT THE AUTHORS

Tim and Debbie Bishop have coauthored four books about their midlife launch into marriage, cross-country bicycle touring, and other matters of faith and inspiration. *Two Are Better: Midlife Newlyweds Bicycle Coast to Coast* captures the story behind the stories, while *Bicycle Touring How-To: What We Learned* shares their knowledge with bicycle touring wannabes. Now, *Wheels of Wisdom: Life Lessons for the Restless Spirit* and *Metaphors in Motion: Wisdom from the Open Road* convey some deeper truths that apply to virtually any life pursuit.

The Bishops have served as volunteer Hope Coaches for TheHopeLine, a nonprofit organization that seeks to reach, rescue, and restore hurting teens and young adults. They are available for speaking engagements about their touring and life experiences. They blog periodically at openroadpress.com.

In addition to consulting for small businesses, Tim Bishop has written *Hedging Demystified: How to Balance Risk and Protect Profit*, a book that explains hedging concepts in easy-to-understand language with practical examples. He has over thirty years of business experience and blogs on hedging at http://hedging.openroadpress.com.

ABOUT THE AUTHORS

Debbie Bishop has taught for over twenty-eight years. She has a passion for reading and seeing that young people do it well. She also has a strong interest in recovery issues and encouraging others with her own triumphs over such struggles earlier in her life. She is a featured author in *Love is Out There* by Melissa Williams-Pope, in which she relates her own story of finding love later than most. Debbie has also volunteered as a facilitator for findingbalance.com, an online support group dedicated to helping women who are struggling with eating disorders.

If you enjoyed *Metaphors in Motion,* wait until you see what's in

Wheels of Wisdom

Life Lessons for the Restless Spirit

By Tim and Debbie Bishop

Recognized eight times in book award contests

First place in:
- Inspiration
- Devotional
- Christian Nonfiction
- Christian Inspirational

Looking for more out of life?

After three tours totaling over 10,000 miles, Tim and Debbie Bishop have discovered wisdom and truth from the seat of a bicycle. In *Wheels of Wisdom*, the authors share the life lessons they learned on the open road.

When you're looking for enlightenment, you can find it almost anywhere, be it from watching two herons saunter across a Florida road, pedaling to a dead-end in a Kentucky tobacco field, or observing eagles flying overhead in Montana. In each lesson of this book, you'll find practical insights, inspiration, and encouragement—along with personal reflection questions that will help you:

- Adopt the right mind-set
- Conquer fear, worry, and inaction
- Overcome obstacles
- Relish life's journey

Certain principles are universal whether you are bicycling across America or chasing your own lifelong dream.

You may be continuing your education, connecting with new people, looking to change jobs, or simply wondering about your future. Wherever you are in life, *Wheels of Wisdom* will give you a fresh perspective and new motivation for your own adventure. Not only will you encounter meaningful truth as you travel vicariously to new places and meet new people, you'll also experience some genuine "God moments" and have some fun on the way.

So, pack up your dreams and passions and come enjooy the ride. It's time to learn on the open road!

You'll find *Wheels of Wisdom: Life Lessons for the Restless Spirit* online or at a bookseller near you.

Wheels of Wisdom Accolades

	"A road map for life . . . incorporates faith without unnecessary preaching." – *Publishers Weekly*
	Selected twice as a "Featured Deal" on Bookbub

Book Awards	Placement	Category	Contest
	Winner	Inspiration	National Indie Excellence Awards
	Gold medal	Devotional	Readers' Favorite Int'l Book Awards
	Winner	Christian Nonfiction	Next Generation Indie Book Awards
	Winner	Christian Inspirational	Best Book Awards
	Bronze medal	Devotional	Illumination Book Awards
	Semifinalist (1 of 20)	Nonfiction	Kindle eBook Awards
	Finalist (1 of 5)	Inspirational Nonfiction	Next Generation Indie Book Awards
	Bronze medal	Adult NF Pers. E-book	Independent Publisher (IPPY) Awards

Order from Open Road Press today!

Two Are Better

Midlife Newlyweds Bicycle Coast to Coast

By Tim and Debbie Bishop

After fifty-two years of life, Tim and Debbie Bishop finally found in each other that special someone for whom they'd been searching. In only ten weeks, they moved from marriage proposal and wedding to Tim's "retirement" and relocation to embarking on the cycling adventure of a lifetime. *Two Are Better* captures the joy and excitement of their odyssey.

Two Are Better: Midlife Newlyweds Bicycle Coast to Coast is a full-color, 208-page, 6" x 9" paperback book published by Open Road Press, including over 100 color photos of the Bishops' honeymoon tour across America. Learn the inspiring story, be challenged to make your own dreams come true, and enjoy a vicarious adventure across a beautiful land.

Also available in e-book formats.

Bicycle Touring How-To

What We Learned

By Tim and Debbie Bishop

Have you ever thought about touring long distance by bicycle? Discover the secrets of a successful bicycle tour in *Bicycle Touring How-To: What We Learned*.

Bicycle Touring How-To is all about learning how to bicycle tour from the ground up–and quickly—because that's just what authors Tim and Debbie Bishop did when they ventured across country after marrying. *"How-To"* contains tips on equipment, security, pre- and post-trip logistics, the daily routine, technology, and much more. You'll even learn how much a tour can cost and how to reduce expenses.

The knowledge expands from the e-book to the Internet with many web links to clarify technical terms, to provide more information on equipment, and to illustrate sample journals, maps, and logs. The e-book contains 19 color photos. *Bicycle Touring How-To* is now available in print.

Written in a conversational style with practicality in mind, this book will enhance your touring experience, whether you choose to tour on a skinny saddle over hill and dale or vicariously from the comfort of your living room recliner.

Order online at www.openroadpress.com

ABOUT OPEN ROAD PRESS

What you do get when you combine faith, life experience, second chances, and thousands of miles of self-supported bicycle touring throughout America?

Inspiration • Hope • Encouragement

Adventure • Fun • Entertainment

You also get uplifting books that share the journey and what it teaches the willing traveler, including an eight-time award winner. *Wheels of Wisdom: Life Lessons for the Restless Spirit* has won four first-place book awards–in Inspiration, Devotional, Christian Nonfiction, and Christian Inspirational. Publishers Weekly dubbed it "a road map for life."

Check out our books at openroadpress.com. Take up the challenge to make meaning and adventure vital parts of your daily life.

Open Road Press • Love and Life by Bicycle

Questions, comments, and feedback are always welcome at openroadpress.com. We will do our best to respond to all constructive comments and questions.

www.ingramcontent.com/pod-product-compliance
Lightning Source LLC
Chambersburg PA
CBHW052030290426
44112CB00014B/2455